WATCHMEN PRAYERS

Compiled by
Israel Mandate Intercessors

Watchmen Prayers

Copyright © 2009 Israel Mandate Intercessors
3535 East Red Bridge Road
Kansas City, MO 64137

Unless otherwise noted, Scripture quotations are from The Holy Bible, English Standard Version®, copyright © 2001 by Crossway Bibles, a publishing ministry of Good News Publishers. Used by permission. All rights reserved.

Scriptures marked NKJV are from the New King James Version. Copyright © 1982 by Thomas Nelson, Inc. Used by permission. All rights reserved.

Scripture marked NIV is from the HOLY BIBLE, NEW INTERNATIONAL VERSION®. Copyright © 1973, 1978, 1984 International Bible Society. Used by permission of Zondervan. All rights reserved.

Printed by Corporate Document Services
9095 Bond Street
Overland Park, KS 66214

ISBN 0-9766412-2-4

Introduction

This book is an invitation to you to join in shaping the destiny of millions of Jewish people and the nation of Israel by "standing in the gap" until all Israel turns to the Lord.

The Hebrew name for Jesus, Yeshua, is used throughout as well as Messiah in place of Christ.

DAY 1

That the God of our Lord Jesus Christ, the Father of glory, may give you a spirit of wisdom and of revelation in the knowledge of him.

Ephesians 1:17

Praying for Israel does not come naturally. Many watchmen on the wall (intercessors) for Zion's sake will testify that God Himself first gave them revelation concerning Israel that set them on the wall for the nation of Israel and the Jewish people.

PRAYER STARTER

Father, I desire to know Your heart for Israel. Give me a spirit of wisdom and revelation concerning both the people and the land of Israel.

NIGHT 1

Now therefore, if I have found favor in your sight, please show me now your ways, that I may know you in order to find favor in your sight. Consider too that this nation is your people.

Exodus 33:13

Moses did not separate his desire to understand God from his desire that God would continue to see Israel as His people. Israel is the means by which God has chosen to reveal Himself to humanity. He has written His Name on them. If you want to know God better, seek to understand His dealings with Israel. Understanding God's dealings with Israel is a door to understanding God.

PRAYER STARTER
God, fill me with the knowledge of Your will in all wisdom and understanding, which the Spirit gives (Colossians 1:9).

DAY 2

On your walls, O Jerusalem, I have set watchmen; all the day and all the night they shall never be silent. You who put the LORD in remembrance, take no rest.
                                               Isaiah 62:6

Being a watchman on the wall for Jerusalem is a wonderful assignment and is one in which God Himself takes special interest. He is so passionate about this assignment that He commands His watchmen to give Him no rest until He restores Jerusalem.

PRAYER STARTER
Lord, here I am. Set me firmly on the wall of intercession for Your people Israel and Your city Jerusalem. Give me grace to stand firm, mature and fully confident as I devote myself completely to Your will (Colossians 4:12).

NIGHT 2

God is in the midst of her, she shall not be moved; God shall help her, just at the break of dawn.
Psalm 46:5 (NKJV)

Jerusalem has been chosen by God as His own, as the "city of the Great King" (Matthew 5:35). Her destiny is to house the majestic, uncreated God of the universe and to be the immovable city from which He rules the earth. Thus, her destiny is to be established forever. Even when the nations rage against her, God will come to help her at the perfect hour, just at the break of dawn.

PRAYER STARTER

Father, we trust Your leadership. Your decisions are for our own good and for the good of the entire planet. Your timing is always perfect. As we wait for Your deliverance and the fulfillment of Your promises to the nation of Israel, establish our hearts on the immutability of Your Word. You will help her. You will rescue her from all her enemies. Thank You, for choosing Jerusalem as the place of Your reign. We ask for her deliverance and that she would be prepared to receive You as her King. Yeshua, return to Jerusalem to shine the light of Your face upon her like the breaking forth of the morning light.

DAY 3

For "everyone who calls on the name of the Lord will be saved." How then will they call on him in whom they have not believed? And how are they to believe in him of whom they have never heard? And how are they to hear without someone preaching? And how are they to preach unless they are sent? As it is written, "How beautiful are the feet of those who preach the good news!"
Romans 10:13–15

Israel has a population of more than seven million people, of whom seventy-five percent are Jewish Israelis (5.5 million), but there are only 10,000 Jews who believe Yeshua is Messiah (Messianic believers). Although these ones are accorded the title of "true Israel" by God, their families and friends often reject them as no longer being Jewish. They may well face unemployment, poverty, and ostracism by close family. To stand for Yeshua is not easy. But, with the ratio of believer to non-believer among the Jewish population being 1:550, these believers represent the hope of their nation.

PRAYER STARTER

Thank You, Father, that when Yeshua came to sit at Your right hand, You sent the Holy Spirit to live in our hearts. We pray that Messianic believers in Israel would feel the presence of the Holy Spirit day by day; that they would be strengthened by Him in their inner being to stand each day for Yeshua, emboldened to cry out for the fullness of life in God in the face of persecution. Father, give them Your heart for the lost, make the feet of Jewish believers in Israel beautiful (Isaiah 52:10); let them be shod with the readiness that comes from the gospel of peace (Ephesians 6:15).

NIGHT 3

Only let your manner of life be worthy of the gospel of Christ, so that whether I come and see you or am absent, I may hear of you that you are standing firm in one spirit, with one mind striving side by side for the faith of the gospel, and not frightened in anything by your opponents. This is a clear sign to them of their destruction, but of your salvation, and that from God.

Philippians 1:27–28

Praying for believers, especially Messianic believers, in Israel is important. The operation and visitation of the Spirit in Israel is a vital part of releasing the great end-time harvest among the nations (Ezekiel 36:23–36).

PRAYER STARTER

Father, I pray for those living in Israel who love Your Son. Make them one as You and the Son are one. Let them be united with the Godhead so that the world may believe that You sent Your Son (John 17:21).

DAY 4

And the LORD said to Moses, "I have seen this people, and behold, it is a stiff-necked people. Now therefore let me alone, that my wrath may burn hot against them and I may consume them, in order that I may make a great nation of you." But Moses implored the LORD his God and said, "O LORD, why does your wrath burn hot against your people, whom you have brought out of the land of Egypt with great power and with a mighty hand? Why should the Egyptians say, 'With evil intent did he bring them out, to kill them in the mountains and to consume them from the face of the earth'? Turn from your burning anger and relent from this disaster against your people. Remember Abraham, Isaac, and Israel, your servants, to whom you swore by your own self, and said to them, 'I will multiply your offspring as the stars of heaven, and all this land that I have promised I will give to your offspring, and they shall inherit it forever.'" And the LORD relented from the disaster that he had spoken of bringing on his people.

Exodus 32:9–14

Replacement theology is the belief that God is finished with Israel and the Church has replaced Israel in God's plan. Moses, the great intercessor for Israel, was given the opportunity to be made into a great nation in place of all the other Israelites. Yet, for the sake of God's Name (character and reputation), he chose to intercede for them instead.

PRAYER STARTER

Father, I ask that people across the world who believe in replacement theology will be given passion for Your Name. Make them become great intercessors for Israel. I am grateful for Your faithfulness to Israel.

NIGHT 4

I am speaking the truth in Christ—I am not lying; my conscience bears me witness in the Holy Spirit—that I have great sorrow and unceasing anguish in my heart. For I could wish that I myself were accursed and cut off from Christ for the sake of my brothers, my kinsmen according to the flesh. They are Israelites, and to them belong the adoption, the glory, the covenants, the giving of the law, the worship, and the promises.

Romans 9:1–4

Paul makes it clear that he is getting ready to make a stunning announcement. Then he proposes an exchange: he spends eternity in the lake of fire and all Israel spends eternity in heaven. This is an intense verse! Especially when you consider that these words were penned under the unction of the Holy Spirit and reflect the anguish in God's heart for His ancient people. If this is how God feels about the Jewish people, should we not desire to align our heart with His?

PRAYER STARTER

O Yeshua, please come and awaken my heart to be in unity with Yours over Your desire to see the Jewish people set free, saved, and walking in the fullness of their holy inheritance. Give me your heart for Israel until all Israel becomes a praise in the earth.

DAY 5

But if some of the branches were broken off, and you, although a wild olive shoot, were grafted in among the others and now share in the nourishing root of the olive tree, do not be arrogant toward the branches. If you are, remember it is not you who support the root, but the root that supports you. Then you will say, "Branches were broken off so that I might be grafted in." That is true. They were broken off because of their unbelief, but you stand fast through faith . . . And even they, if they do not continue in their unbelief, will be grafted in, for God has the power to graft them in again. For if you were cut from what is by nature a wild olive tree, and grafted, contrary to nature, into a cultivated olive tree, how much more will these, the natural branches, be grafted back into their own olive tree.
Romans 11:17–24

The roots of Christianity are Jewish. The apostles were all Jewish and virtually every book of the Bible was written by Jewish people. Likewise, Yeshua Himself is Jewish. By grace God made a way for Gentiles (non-Jews) to be a part of the olive tree; many Jews would walk in unbelief and so be cut off and we, the wild branches, grafted in. Yet God's Word says, if they (the Jewish people) do not persist in their lack of belief, they will be grafted in again.

PRAYER STARTER

Father, I see the natural branches separated from You and I ache for them. Holy Spirit, bring to their remembrance the faith of their forefather Abraham, who believed and it was counted to him as righteousness (Genesis 15:6, Psalm 106:31). Please graft Your people back in.

NIGHT 5

That the God of our Lord Jesus Christ, the Father of glory, may give you a spirit of wisdom and revelation in the knowledge of him.
Ephesians 1:17

As Gentile believers, we so often think that we have all the answers! In Romans 11:18, Paul warns us not to "boast against the branches" which are Israel, and in verse 20 he urges us to "not be haughty, but fear." The fear of the Lord is the beginning of wisdom. As we pray that the eyes of the Jews would be opened to the man Yeshua and their ears unstopped, may we remember that we as Gentile believers do not have full revelation of the mysteries of God.

PRAYER STARTER
Father, have mercy on us, Your Gentile church, and forgive us for our arrogance regarding Israel. Release to us a spirit of wisdom and revelation regarding Your heart for Your people. Open our eyes to see them as You see them, and our ears to hear what You have to say about the people on the earth that You call the apple of Your eye.

DAY 6

The king loved Esther more than all the women, and she won grace and favor in his sight more than all the virgins.
Esther 2:17

Favor with God and man is given for the purpose of intercession. Moses understood that he was in a position of favor with God, and from that place he cried out for Israel (Exodus 33:13). Joseph was his father's favorite and saved the descendents of Abraham (Genesis 45:7). Esther had favor with an earthly king and was able to preserve her people (Esther 8:6–8). Through the blood of the Lamb, the only begotten of the Father, we can all stand confidently in a position of favor.

PRAYER STARTER
Heavenly King, I have been born for such a time as this. I was born to intercede. Save Your people Israel!

NIGHT 6

Hear, O daughter, and consider, and incline your ear: forget your people and your father's house, and the king will desire your beauty. Since he is your lord, bow to him.
Psalm 45:10–11

Abraham was told to leave his father's house and go to a land God would show him. Jacob found his God after leaving his father's house and Joseph achieved his destiny only by leaving his father's house. Moses left his people and his father's house and found God in the desert.

PRAYER STARTER
Almighty God, let Israel consider everything a loss because of the supreme value of knowing the Messiah Yeshua as Lord. Give them grace to give up everything and regard it all as garbage in order to gain Messiah and be found in union with Him, not having any righteousness of their own (father's house) but having a righteousness from God based on faith (Philippians 3:8–9).

DAY 7

O Jerusalem, Jerusalem, the city that kills the prophets and stones those who are sent to it! How often would I have gathered your children together as a hen gathers her brood under her wings, and you would not! See, your house is left to you desolate. For I tell you, you will not see me again, until you say, "Blessed is he who comes in the name of the Lord."

Matthew 23:37–39

Yeshua wept over the city of Jerusalem because in their search for joy and freedom, the leadership of Israel had rejected the only King who could give them joy and freedom. In their search for eternal life, they had rejected the source of life. Yeshua gave them over to their choice: they would not see the answer to their prophetic dreams until they welcomed Him back.

PRAYER STARTER

Father, raise up a generation in Israel who will welcome Yeshua back as their rightful King. Open the eyes of the hearts among the people of the land, that the Jewish people could recognize their Messiah and welcome Him back.

NIGHT 7

For the LORD has chosen Zion; he has desired it for his dwelling place: "This is my resting place forever; here I will dwell, for I have desired it."

Psalm 132:13–14

When writing this Psalm, David was given insight into the deep longing and ache of God Himself. The God of the universe desires to live in Zion!

PRAYER STARTER

Yeshua, let me partner with the deep longings of Your heart in this late hour. Let me invest in prayer towards the redemption of Israel. For You said You would not return to Israel until the Jewish leaders say, "Blessed is He who comes in the Name of the Lord."

DAY 8

I will wait for the LORD, who is hiding his face from the house of Jacob, and I will hope in him. Behold, I and the children whom the LORD has given me are signs and wonders in Israel from the LORD of hosts, who dwells on Mount Zion.

Isaiah 8:17–18

Three important truths of our watchmen role can be found in this scripture. First, as watchmen our job is to wait. This is an active waiting which watches in anticipation. Second, God is hiding His face from the house of Jacob; in other words, partial blindness has been placed on Israel by God Himself (Romans 11:25). Third, we can have normal lives: have children, jobs, etc., and still be watchmen for Israel. As we live our lives and yet carry the salvation of Israel as one of our greatest desires, we will become for Israel signs and wonders from our Lord.

PRAYER STARTER

Lord, here I am waiting for You to lift the veil and show Your face to Your people Israel. Let them see the face of Yeshua, the exact image of the invisible God (Colossians 1:15). Lord, pour out Your Spirit in me and my "children," that we may be signs and wonders pointing the Jewish people to their Messiah, Yeshua.

NIGHT 8

Lest you be wise in your own sight, I want you to understand this mystery, brothers: a partial hardening has come upon Israel, until the fullness of the Gentiles has come in. And in this way all Israel will be saved, as it is written, "The Deliverer will come from Zion, he will banish ungodliness from Jacob."

Romans 11:25–26

As Gentiles, we should be eternally grateful that God saw it fit to make Israel's heart stony so we could enter into our fullness. At the same time, it should grieve our hearts that God deemed this necessary. Our right response should be a heart's cry for the fullness to come to the Gentiles—not for some self-serving reason, but so that all Israel will be saved.

PRAYER STARTER

Father, I pray for the fullness to come to the Gentile church so all Israel will be saved. For this reason, I fall on my knees before You, the Father, from whom every family in heaven and on earth receives its character. I pray that from the treasures of Your glory You will empower the Gentiles with inner strength by Your Spirit so that Messiah may live in our hearts through faith. Also, I pray that we would be rooted and grounded in love so that we, with all God's people, will be given strength to grasp the breadth, length, height, and depth of Messiah's love—yes, to know it even though it is beyond all knowing—so that we will be filled with all the fullness of God (Ephesians 3:14–19).

DAY 9

Brothers, my heart's desire and prayer to God for them is that they may be saved.

Romans 10:1

Paul knew how to pray, and his prayers were deep and often eloquent in wording (see Ephesians 3:16–19). And yet when it comes to Israel, Paul's recorded prayers are short. Possibly his prayers for Israel were more of a groan or cry. His desperate prayer for the salvation of Israel came from a heart that was willing to be cursed if it would save some of his Jewish brothers (Romans 9:3).

PRAYER STARTER

Please, Lord, save! Please, Lord, rescue! Blessed is He who comes in the Name of the Lord (Psalm 118:25–26).

NIGHT 9

The Lord is my shepherd; I shall not want.
Psalm 23:1

And I have other sheep that are not of this fold. I must bring them also, and they will listen to my voice. So there will be one flock, one shepherd.
John 10:16

Yeshua said of His ministry, "I came for the lost sheep of Israel." As ones who are now part of the Good Shepherd's flock we should long for His flock to be complete. Our bleating (voices) should be heard calling out for the sheep who are not yet in the fold.

PRAYER STARTER

Good Shepherd of Israel, gather and guard Your sheep (Jeremiah 31:10). Search for Your sheep and seek them out. As a shepherd seeks out his flock when he is among his sheep that have been scattered, seek out Your sheep, and rescue them from all places where they were scattered on a day of clouds and thick darkness (Ezekiel 34:11–12).

DAY 10

Let me sing for my beloved my love song concerning his vineyard: My beloved had a vineyard on a very fertile hill. He dug it and cleared it of stones, and planted it with choice vines; he built a watchtower in the midst of it, and hewed out a wine vat in it; and he looked for it to yield grapes.

Isaiah 5:1–2

As branches grafted into the natural vine and in love with the One who owns the vineyard, we should sing for Israel's return. Carrying Israel in prayer and song is an awesome opportunity to have intimate partnership with Yeshua.

PRAYER STARTER

God Almighty, post me as a watchman in the watchtower of the vineyard of Israel and give me songs to sing over her. Permit me to work with You in clearing a way for Your people. Use me to build up the highway, clear away the stones, and raise up a banner for Your people (Isaiah 62:10).

NIGHT 10

In days to come Jacob shall take root, Israel shall blossom and put forth shoots and fill the whole world with fruit.
                                            Isaiah 27:6

Israel's prophetic destiny is to be chief of the nations. Nations will come to Zion, streaming to the goodness of the Lord once Israel is restored (Jeremiah 31:12).

PRAYER STARTER

Father, we sing with joy for Jacob and we shout for the chief of the nations! We proclaim Your praise and say, "O Lord save Your people, the remnant of Israel!" (Jeremiah 31:7).

DAY 11

For as the rain and the snow come down from heaven and do not return there but water the earth, making it bring forth and sprout, giving seed to the sower and bread to the eater, so shall my word be that goes out from my mouth; it shall not return to me empty, but it shall accomplish that which I purpose, and shall succeed in the thing for which I sent it.

Isaiah 55:10–11

The Torah (first five books of the Bible), which contains God's redemptive plan and imagery of Yeshua, is read weekly and even daily by many Jewish people. We can trust that His Word, which has been read over the centuries in synagogues and yeshivas (academies for the advanced study of Jewish texts), will accomplish its intent in the hearts of the readers. Reading the Torah along with the Jewish people and asking God to fulfill His Word is a great way to pray for Israel.

PRAYER STARTER

I pray that the Word of the Lord may run swiftly and be glorified in synagogues, yeshivas, homes and wherever it is read (2 Thessalonians 3:1).

NIGHT 11

Is Ephraim my dear son? Is he my darling child? For as often as I speak against him, I do remember him still. Therefore my heart yearns for him; I will surely have mercy on him, declares the LORD.
Jeremiah 31:20

The ache in the heart of the One (Yeshua) who is always interceding for His people (Hebrews 7:25) is very real and constant. There are many young men and women in yeshivas for whom the Lord aches. They study the *Torah* and are genuine in their search for truth. To date, they have not found Him—the Way, the Truth, and the Life.

PRAYER STARTER

Lord, as yeshiva students search Your Word, call them to mind. Show them favor and reveal Your Son to them. Father, we ask You to release a spirit of wisdom and revelation to the multitude of young adults in Israel. Visit them like You did Peter, James, and John. Speak to them, open Your Word to them, come disciple them.

DAY 12

So I ask, did they stumble in order that they might fall? By no means! Rather through their trespass salvation has come to the Gentiles, so as to make Israel jealous.
Romans 11:11

Jealousy is an emotion that occurs when someone sees another person possessing something that is rightfully theirs, like a jealous husband when his wife gives attention to another man. The Gentiles have been given the responsibility to provoke the Jews to jealousy. We, the Gentiles believers, need wisdom to know how to make them jealous. We need to know what has been given to us, that Jewish people will recognize our gifts as belonging to them too.

PRAYER STARTER

Father, thank You for giving Your Gentile believers gifts that were given irrevocably and still belong to the Jewish people. Help Your Church to know what these gifts are and to put them on display with humility as we relate to the Jewish people.

NIGHT 12

Now I am speaking to you Gentiles. Inasmuch then as I am an apostle to the Gentiles, I magnify my ministry in order somehow to make my fellow Jews jealous, and thus save some of them . . . I want you to understand this mystery, brothers: a partial hardening has come upon Israel, until the fullness of the Gentiles has come in. And in this way all Israel will be saved.
Romans 11:13–26

The apostle Paul had a surprising evangelistic strategy. He labored for the salvation of Gentile people in order to provoke his Jewish brethren. Paul believed that when the Gentile peoples discovered the wonders of the God of Israel, they would provoke the Jews to jealousy, who, in turn, would come to find salvation in Yeshua. Among all the Gentile peoples on the earth capable of provoking the Jews to jealousy, probably none is more strategic than the group who lives among them: the Palestinians, the vast majority of whom are Muslims. Consider the effects of an outpouring of salvation among the Palestinians who have a history of both suffering violence from and perpetrating violence against Israel.

PRAYER STARTER

Father, I lift before You the Palestinian people. I ask You to make known to them Your goodness and release revelation of Your Son Yeshua, the Savior of the world. God, I ask You to release an outpouring of salvation among them, that they would come to love the God of Israel. And I ask that they would be filled with compassion for the "lost sheep of the house of Israel" (Matthew 10:6, 15:24) and labor for their salvation.

DAY 13

And you shall set the two stones on the shoulder pieces of the ephod, as stones of remembrance for the sons of Israel. And Aaron shall bear their names before the LORD on his two shoulders for remembrance . . . So Aaron shall bear the names of the sons of Israel in the breastpiece of judgment on his heart, when he goes into the Holy Place, to bring them to regular remembrance before the LORD.

Exodus 28:12, 29

Yeshua purchased us with His blood to be priests (Revelation 5:9–10). As priests before God, we are to be clothed with a burden for Israel. We can trust our Great High Priest's words that His burden is easy.

PRAYER STARTER

Lord, like the priests of old, give me grace to carry Israel on my shoulders. Place Your yoke upon me. Give me grace to carry the tribes of Israel on my heart as well.

NIGHT 13

My covenant with him [Levi] was one of life and peace, and I gave them to him. It was a covenant of fear, and he feared me. He stood in awe of my name. True instruction was in his mouth, and no wrong was found on his lips. He walked with me in peace and uprightness, and he turned many from iniquity.

Malachi 2:5–6

A true priesthood will be marked with the fear of the Lord and truth in their mouths. Israel and all of humanity desperately need a people entirely given to God (Numbers 8:16), a people in covenant with God.

PRAYER STARTER

Father, release the fear of God into the hearts of believers, especially Jewish ones, in the land of Israel. Release the lightning and thunder from Your Throne to strike their hearts (Revelation 4:5) with Your majesty, that they might live in awe before You. Release Your presence and holy dread that makes them tremble before You. Unite their hearts to Your heart and Word, and put the true *torah* (instruction) in their mouths that they would turn many away from sin.

DAY 14

For the Lord has chosen Zion; he has desired it for his dwelling place. "This is my resting place forever; here I will dwell, for I have desired it."

Psalm 132:13–14

There will be a day when God splits the sky and the New Jerusalem descends like a bride (Revelation 21:10). On that day there will be no more tears, sorrow or pain, and we will rest with our God.

PRAYER STARTER

The Spirit and the Bride say come. Come to Jerusalem and reign. Come to Your resting place, You and the ark of Your might (Psalm 132:9).

NIGHT 14

I will tell of the decree: The LORD said to me, "You are my Son; today I have begotten you. Ask of me, and I will make the nations your heritage, and the ends of the earth your possession."

Psalm 2:7–8

The eternal God and Father of all decrees that Yeshua the Messiah will rule the nations of the earth from Jerusalem. This is our great hope, as all things will be renewed when Yeshua finally physically rules on the earth from Mount Zion.

PRAYER STARTER

Father, let Your kingdom come quickly on the earth as it is in heaven. Let the people of Israel rejoice at the coming of their King, Yeshua the Messiah.

DAY 15

Then Boaz said to his young man who was in charge of the reapers, "Whose young woman is this?" . . . Then she fell on her face, bowing to the ground, and said to him, "Why have I found favor in your eyes, that you should take notice of me, since I am a foreigner?" But Boaz answered her, "All that you have done for your mother-in-law since the death of your husband has been fully told to me, and how you left your father and mother and your native land and came to a people that you did not know before. The LORD repay you for what you have done, and a full reward be given you by the LORD, the God of Israel, under whose wings you have come to take refuge!"

Ruth 2:5, 10–12

We are called to be like Ruth and yoke ourselves to Naomi (Israel) even if she is bitter. We are to seek her well-being. As we do, we will capture the eye of their Kinsman-Redeemer, Yeshua the Messiah.

PRAYER STARTER

Father, as I pray for Israel, let me comprehend the height, the width, the length, and the depth of Your love. Yes let me know this love, even though it is beyond all knowing, that I may be filled with the measure of all fullness (Ephesians 3:18–19). As I stand with Israel, let me hear You say, "You have captured my heart" (Song of Solomon 4:9).

NIGHT 15

Comfort, comfort my people, says your God. Speak tenderly to Jerusalem, and cry to her that her warfare is ended, that her iniquity is pardoned, that she has received from the LORD's hand double for all her sins.
Isaiah 40:1–2

The Holy Spirit, who lives in each of us who believe, is the Comforter. On the cross, Yeshua paid for all guilt, and at His hand the desire of the Lord has prospered (Isaiah 53:10). Jerusalem will indeed receive their portion when Yeshua returns to reign as King of kings and Lord of lords from Mount Zion.

PRAYER STARTER
Father, I pray that Israel would accept the gift of Your Son and all that He has completed for them. Let them receive their portion and know Your presence.

DAY 16

Behold, the LORD has proclaimed to the end of the earth: Say to the daughter of Zion, "Behold, your salvation comes; behold, his reward is with him, and his recompense before him."

Isaiah 62:11

The Lord has spoken clearly the message His watchmen are to speak to the daughter of Zion—the message about the One who is Salvation, the One who rewards, and the One who brings justice: Yeshua.

PRAYER STARTER
Father, I sign up not only to be a watchman but also a messenger. Let me speak the words You give me to the people of Israel. Raise up many watchmen and messengers for Israel.

NIGHT 16

For thus says the LORD: "Sing aloud with gladness for Jacob, and raise shouts for the chief of the nations; proclaim, give praise, and say, 'O LORD, save your people, the remnant of Israel.'"

Jeremiah 31:7

The Lord has called Israel the "chief of the nations" and has commissioned us to proclaim, "You saved Your people the remnant of Israel." That Israel is chosen to be chief of the nations should cause us to sing with joy and praise the Lord for His faithfulness to them. After all, they were the first to be made God's children; the glory of God has been with them; the covenants are theirs, and likewise the giving of the Torah, the temple services, the promises, and the patriarchs; and from them came the Messiah who is over all (Romans 9:4–5).

PRAYER STARTER

Lord, we do sing for joy for Jacob and praise You for Your faithfulness in always preserving a remnant of Israel. You tell us to pray for our leaders, so we do pray for them. We ask that You would count them worthy of this calling as the chief of the nations and give them grace to believe in the One who is perfect in His love and leadership, Your Son Yeshua. Through Him alone will they be able to walk in their calling.

DAY 17

And the scroll of the prophet Isaiah was given to him. He unrolled the scroll and found the place where it was written, "The Spirit of the Lord is upon me, because he has anointed me to proclaim good news to the poor. He has sent me to proclaim liberty to the captives and recovering of sight to the blind, to set at liberty those who are oppressed, to proclaim the year of the Lord's favor."
Luke 4:17–19

During Yeshua's trial the Jewish leaders said, "Let His blood be on our heads" (Matthew 27:25). Think of the power of this curse. Within the same generation it was uttered, Jerusalem and the Temple were destroyed and the Jewish people were sent into exile. Since then the Jewish people have suffered in every country. Yet the blood of Yeshua was not intended as a curse. Rather, it was the key to God's redemptive plan.

PRAYER STARTER
I proclaim that the blood of Yeshua is upon the Jewish people and upon their children for good and not for evil. I proclaim the power of that blood to bring blessing to the people of Israel and to the whole world.

NIGHT 17

Now the LORD said to Abram, "Go from your country and your kindred and your father's house to the land that I will show you. And I will make of you a great nation, and I will bless you and make your name great, so that you will be a blessing. I will bless those who bless you, and him who dishonors you I will curse, and in you all the families of the earth shall be blessed."

Genesis 12:1–3

The Lord promised to bless those who bless Israel. Praying for Israel is a sure way to bless them.

PRAYER STARTER

I bless the people of Israel with the blessing the Lord commanded Aaron to use: "The Lord bless you, and keep you; the Lord make His face shine on you, and be gracious to you; the Lord lift up His countenance on you, and give you peace" (Numbers 6:24–26).

DAY 18

Delight yourself in the LORD, and he will give you the desires of your heart.

Psalm 37:4

If you want to get a heart for Israel, then delight yourself in the Lord. In that place of delight, He will place His longings for Israel in you.

PRAYER STARTER

Father, let this prayer become a deep reality in me: "My heart's deepest desire and prayer for Israel is for their salvation" (Romans 10:1).

NIGHT 18

Remember, O LORD, in David's favor, all the hardships he endured, how he swore to the LORD and vowed to the Mighty One of Jacob, "I will not enter my house or get into my bed, I will not give sleep to my eyes or slumber to my eyelids, until I find a place for the LORD, a dwelling place for the Mighty One of Jacob."
Psalms 132:1–5

It was not enough for David to seek the Lord privately and experience the pleasures of gazing on His beauty. He wanted a demonstration of God's presence in Israel for all the nations to see so they would fear the God of Israel. So intensely did this zeal burn within him that he swore to the Mighty One that he would not pursue his own personal comfort until there was a habitation for God in Israel.

PRAYER STARTER
Father, fill houses of prayer and congregations in Jerusalem and throughout Israel with zealous believers, especially Jewish ones. Let there be a company of people who give up legitimate pleasures in order to create a place for You.

DAY 19

In that day there will be a highway from Egypt to Assyria, and Assyria will come into Egypt, and Egypt into Assyria, and the Egyptians will worship with the Assyrians. In that day Israel will be the third with Egypt and Assyria, a blessing in the midst of the earth, whom the LORD of hosts has blessed, saying, "Blessed be Egypt my people, and Assyria the work of my hands, and Israel my inheritance."
                                                    Isaiah 19:23–25

"On that day" is the language used to describe the end-times. The wound of Ishmael (the Arab people) caused when Abraham sent him away has been carried in the heart of the Arab people over thousands of years. Yet the Father will come to Egypt (an Arab nation) and call them "my people." In that moment they will know the love of the Father and also the Father's heart towards the sons of Isaac (Jewish people). They will be set free to love the Son who willingly offered himself (like Isaac) and to love His heritage (the people Israel). *Ishmael* means "the Lord pays attention." He will pray and be heard! And so all Israel will be saved.

PRAYER STARTER

Father, call the Egyptians "Your people." Bring salvation to the neighbors of Israel. Let them know the hope of their calling. Heal their wounded heart and give them grace to cry out for Israel's salvation, for this is the destiny of Ishmael and his descendents.

NIGHT 19

May the God of endurance and encouragement grant you to live in such harmony with one another, in accord with Christ Jesus, that together you may with one voice glorify the God and Father of our Lord Jesus Christ.
                                            Romans 15:5–6

A peaceful relationship between the Jews and Palestinians appears to be a distant dream. After looking at the stand-off between the Jewish people and the Palestinians in Gaza, it is easy to conclude that the answer to this prayer for unity would constitute a genuine miracle from God. However, this tense situation, is a perfect opportunity for believers in Israel to make known the manifold wisdom of God and reveal Yeshua.

PRAYER STARTER
Father, we ask that You would make known the manifold wisdom of God through Jewish and Palestinian believers. Give Jewish and Palestinian followers of Your Son Your spirit of unity among themselves. Unveil a corporate witness of Yeshua through Jews and Palestinians fellowshipping with one another.

DAY 20

Your name shall no longer be called Jacob, but Israel, for you have striven with God and with men, and have prevailed.

Genesis 32:28

Jacob got in a wrestling match with the preincarnate Yeshua and prevailed! Something happened during that wrestling match that defined the nation of Israel. The word *prevailed* means to overcome, to win the victory. Israel will be true to Yeshua's defining word over them and overcome. Great is the reward for those who overcome!

PRAYER STARTER

We call Israel into their destiny to be overcomers. Thank You, Almighty God, that You will give overcomers the right to eat from the tree of life, authority over the nations, hidden manna, and the bright morning star. Thank You that they will be dressed in white and will receive all You have promised to overcomers (Revelation 2 and 3).

NIGHT 20

Then Jacob asked him, "Please tell me your name." But he said, "Why is it that you ask my name?" And there he blessed him. So Jacob called the name of the place Peniel, saying, "For I have seen God face to face, and yet my life has been delivered."

Genesis 32:29–30

One day God will tell Israel the Name of the One who wrestled Jacob: the Name above all names. And at the Name of Yeshua every knee will bow and every tongue confess that Yeshua Messiah is Lord (Philippians 2:10).

PRAYER STARTER

Father, the time has come to glorify Your Son (John 17:1). Speak His Name to the Jewish people that the lost may confess His Name and be saved.

DAY 21

All your allies have forgotten you; they care nothing for you.

                              Jeremiah 30:14 (NIV)

There will be a time when Israel will have no friends among the nations and will find herself alone with her God. This will be by the hand of God. He chooses to encounter His people when they are alone. Jacob was all alone when he wrestled with God. Moses was alone when he first encountered God in the burning bush and then on the mountain when God gave him the law. Additionally, Joseph, who is a type of Yeshua, sent all his servants out before he revealed his identity to his brothers.

PRAYER STARTER

Father, when the time comes that Israel finds herself all alone, I pray it will be a time for her to know You. Let Israel find the place of knowing You and being fully known by You, that she would say, "You are all I have and You are enough."

NIGHT 21

That I may know him and the power of his resurrection, and may share his sufferings, becoming like him in his death, that by any means possible I may attain the resurrection from the dead.
Philippians 3:10–11

For if their rejection means the reconciliation of the world, what will their acceptance mean but life from the dead?
Romans 11:15

We as Gentiles desperately need Israel to know Yeshua. Our eternal destiny is forever linked to theirs. God has seen fit that Israel in their acceptance of Yeshua is the guarantee of life from the dead.

PRAYER STARTER

God of our Lord Yeshua the Messiah, glorious Father, give to Israel a spirit of wisdom and revelation so that they will have full knowledge of Yeshua. I pray that You will give light to the eyes of their hearts, so that they will understand the hope to which they have been called, what rich glories there are in the inheritance You promised Your people and how surpassingly great is Your power working in those who trust You. Let them know the power that You used to raise Messiah from the dead (Ephesians 1:17–20).

DAY 22

For your Maker is your husband, the LORD of hosts is his name; and the Holy One of Israel is your Redeemer, the God of the whole earth he is called.
Isaiah 54:5

Husbands, love your wives, as Christ loved the church and gave himself up for her, that he might sanctify her, having cleansed her by the washing of water with the word.
Ephesians 5:25–26

God intimately understands the human heart that He formed. He knows perfectly how to motivate His people toward holiness. He says in essence, "Turn to Me because I am married to you and because I desire you." The revelation that God loves and desires His people is the single most powerful revelation in the universe; it is the highest motivator for calling people to abandon all else for Him in the final hours of history as the Lord raises up a Bride with a heart after God.

PRAYER STARTER

Once again, God, tell Your people You are a husband to them. Let them hear You call them *Heftzi-Vah* (My delight is in her). Oh that they would call You *Ishi* (my husband). Raise up a bride confident in love within Israel and throughout the Diaspora (Jews living outside Israel).

NIGHT 22

Hear, O Israel: The LORD our God, the LORD is one. You shall love the LORD your God with all your heart and with all your soul and with all your might. And these words that I command you today shall be on your heart.
Deuteronomy 6:4–6

Keeping *torah* (the law) was intended to be a reflection of love for the Lord. With the New Covenant, God has promised to write *torah* on the hearts of His people.

PRAYER STARTER
Father, as You promised, put Your *torah* within the hearts of Your people Israel. Let them all know You, from the least to the greatest (Jeremiah 31:33–34).

DAY 23

Comfort, comfort my people, says your God.
Isaiah 40:1

The children of Abraham, Isaac, and Jacob have been waiting thousands of years for the fulfillment of ancient promises given by the Lord. Scripture says that hope deferred makes the heart sick (Proverbs 13:12). In this late hour of history, many Jewish people have chosen to live for themselves apart from God.

PRAYER STARTER

Father God, reveal Your Son as the comforter and the consolation of Israel. Give Your people the Light of life and hope once again.

NIGHT 23

Then I will remember my covenant with Jacob, and I will remember my covenant with Isaac and my covenant with Abraham, and I will remember the land.
Leviticus 26:42

Thus says the LORD, "If I have not established my covenant with day and night and the fixed order of heaven and earth, then I will reject the offspring of Jacob and David my servant and will not choose one of his offspring to rule over the offspring of Abraham, Isaac, and Jacob. For I will restore their fortunes and will have mercy on them."
Jeremiah 33:25–26

A covenant is a promise given by one party in a position of strength to a weaker party. If the covenant is unconditional, it is binding upon the giver even if the weaker party fails to uphold their part of the agreement. God is a covenant-making and covenant-keeping God. He will not forsake His people.

PRAYER STARTER

Father of glory, bring revelation to those who don't understand the truth concerning Your heart for Israel. You have not rejected Israel. You are true to Your word.

DAY 24

And now, Lord, look upon their threats and grant to your servants to continue to speak your word with all boldness, while you stretch out your hand to heal, and signs and wonders are performed through the name of your holy servant Jesus. And when they had prayed, the place in which they were gathered together was shaken, and they were all filled with the Holy Spirit and continued to speak the word of God with boldness.

Acts 4:29–31

Peter had just been arrested and imprisoned for healing the lame man at the Gate Beautiful and was told that he should not speak or teach in the name of Yeshua. The early disciples' instinctive reaction was to gather together and cry out to God to give them boldness and to continue to heal those that they prayed for. In the face of opposition, they pressed into God. He answered! The place was shaken and the disciples were filled with the Holy Spirit and they spoke the word of God with boldness. So be it for the Messianic believers in Israel!

PRAYER STARTER

Father, shake the prayer meetings of the believers in Israel. Give them boldness in the face of opposition, courage to speak the truth and wisdom as they declare the good news of Yeshua. Raise up an apostolic witness in Israel today. Father of glory, I ask You to release Your power in the city of Jerusalem just as You did 2,000 years ago. Strengthen and empower believers in Israel, that many would be saved through a mighty witness of the gospel.

NIGHT 24

And in the last days it shall be, God declares, that I will pour out my Spirit on all flesh, and your sons and your daughters shall prophesy, and your young men shall see visions, and your old men shall dream dreams; even on my male servants and female servants in those days I will pour out my Spirit, and they shall prophesy. And I will show wonders in the heavens above and signs on the earth below, blood, and fire, and vapor of smoke; the sun shall be turned to darkness and the moon to blood, before the day of the Lord comes, the great and magnificent day. And it shall come to pass that everyone who calls upon the name of the Lord shall be saved.

Acts 2:17–21

The Lord poured out His Spirit 2,000 years ago on the day of Pentecost. His desire is to release this promise through an unprecedented outpouring of His Spirit that will cause thousands of Jews to prophesy and proclaim the glories of Messiah to all of Israel and to the nations of the earth. This will include mighty signs and wonders just before the return of Yeshua.

PRAYER STARTER

Thank You, Lord, for this glorious promise. I believe it and I ask You to pour out Your Spirit today on Israel. Fill the hearts of Jewish believers with the spirit of prophecy, and the testimony of Yeshua, and release mighty signs and wonders unto the salvation of thousands.

DAY 25

He was oppressed, and he was afflicted, yet he opened not his mouth; like a lamb that is led to the slaughter, and like a sheep that before its shearers is silent, so he opened not his mouth . . . Therefore I will divide him a portion with the many, and he shall divide the spoil with the strong, because he poured out his soul to death and was numbered with the transgressors; yet he bore the sin of many, and makes intercession for the transgressors.

Isaiah 53:7, 12

The next day he saw Jesus coming toward him, and said, "Behold, the Lamb of God, who takes away the sin of the world!"

John 1:29

Yeshua will return to the land of Israel to rule and reign as King of the whole earth. Beyond mandatory obedience, Yeshua is worthy of a people in Israel who voluntarily love and obey Him as King.

PRAYER STARTER

Worthy is the Lamb who was slain to receive power, and wealth, and wisdom, and strength, and honor, and glory, and praise (Revelation 5:12). We ask for a great number of His own brethren who will voluntarily love and obey King Yeshua.

NIGHT 25

For Zion's sake I will not keep silent, and for Jerusalem's sake I will not be quiet, until her righteousness goes forth as brightness, and her salvation as a burning torch.

Isaiah. 62:1

But now thus says the LORD, he who created you, O Jacob, he who formed you, O Israel: "Fear not, for I have redeemed you; I have called you by name, you are mine. When you pass through the waters, I will be with you; and through the rivers, they shall not overwhelm you; when you walk through fire you shall not be burned, and the flame shall not consume you. For I am the LORD your God, the Holy One of Israel, your Savior."

Isaiah 43:1–3

Yeshua is Israel's Savior and Redeemer and is zealous to see her shine forth righteousness and be a light to the nations of the earth, as she has revelation of Him as Messiah. Just as God delivered Moses and the Israelites and they passed through on dry ground, and just as Shadrach, Meschach and Abednego were saved from the heat of the fiery furnace, His desire is to save and deliver His chosen people as they call on His Name.

PRAYER STARTER

Lord, let us be zealous for Zion like You are, and let us not grow weary in interceding for Israel with boldness. Reveal Yourself as Israel's only Savior, deliverer and hope of salvation. Strengthen the believers in Israel. Let them take courage and know that You hold them in Your hand and will be their shield, refuge, and peace.

DAY 26

I will surely assemble all of you, O Jacob; I will gather the remnant of Israel; I will set them together like sheep in a fold, like a flock in its pasture, a noisy multitude of men. He who opens the breach goes up before them; they break through and pass the gate, going out by it. Their king passes on before them, the LORD at their head.
Micah 2:12–13

Micah prophesied about a future day when the Messiah would lead Israel with a breaker anointing. In other words, He would help Israel break out of the old way and break open new dimensions of the purpose of God. Yeshua is the ultimate expression of the breaker anointing, the One who breaks open new dimensions of the Spirit for others to enter into. The Holy Spirit is raising up forerunners today who will break out and break through for themselves and others. These ones will be people of one thing (Psalm 27:4), contending for the power of God and fullness of the apostolic faith that had its origins in the Holy Land.

PRAYER STARTER

Holy Spirit, anoint believers in the land of Israel with a breaker anointing. Give them grace to follow the Lamb wherever He goes and open the way for others to follow. Raise up forerunners for God.

NIGHT 26

Then I will gather the remnant of my flock out of all the countries where I have driven them, and I will bring them back to their fold, and they shall be fruitful and multiply. I will set shepherds over them who will care for them, and they shall fear no more, nor be dismayed, neither shall any be missing, declares the LORD.
Jeremiah 23:3–4

The Holy Spirit is raising up shepherds to teach God's people how to live after His own heart. They will feed others from the reality they encounter through their own unyielding pursuit of God. They will only be able to shepherd others because they have given themselves wholly to the great Shepherd, Yeshua.

PRAYER STARTER

Shepherd of Israel, thank You for raising up shepherds after Your own heart. I pray for the shepherds You have raised up among the Jewish people: give them unlimited grace to love You with all their heart, all their soul, all their mind, and all their strength.

DAY 27

I appeal to you therefore, brothers, by the mercies of God, to present your bodies as a living sacrifice, holy and acceptable to God, which is your spiritual worship. Do not be conformed to this world, but be transformed by the renewal of your mind, that by testing you may discern what is the will of God, what is good and acceptable and perfect.
Romans 12:1–2

The most powerful witness one can give sinners is a radiant life demonstrating that the will of God is good, acceptable, and perfect. Unbelievers are looking for contented, fulfilled people who aren't trying to cast off God's restraints, a people who are joyfully abandoned and totally committed to His cause. The Jewish people need to see believers who have turned their backs on the world and given their all to the Messiah who gave everything for them.

PRAYER STARTER

Father, raise up a believing community in Israel who are joyfully abandoned and totally committed to Your cause. Father, teach them Your ways so that they can prove Your good, acceptable, and perfect will in their lives.

NIGHT 27

But the LORD of hosts, him you shall honor as holy. Let him be your fear, and let him be your dread. And he will become a sanctuary and a stone of offense and a rock of stumbling to both houses of Israel, a trap and a snare to the inhabitants of Jerusalem.

Isaiah 8:13–14

The Pharisees and the disciples both misunderstood Yeshua and, consequently, they were both offended. Those who were offended and who turned away from Yeshua when He said, "I am the living bread which came down from heaven" (John 6:51) were not Pharisees but His disciples (followers other than the twelve). Though He taught with great wisdom and did a few mighty works in His hometown, His friends "were offended at Him" (Matthew 13:57). The most commonly used Greek word in the New Testament for *offend* is also translated "to stumble." The Greek word is *skandalizo*, from which our English word *scandal* is derived. By offending people's minds, God revealed the things in their hearts that caused them to stumble. Yeshua is revealed in the Bible not only as the Resurrection and the Life, and the Bread of Life, but also as "the stone of stumbling and the rock of offense" (Isaiah 8:14).

PRAYER STARTER

Father, in Your mercy, reveal any hidden thing within the hearts of believers in the land that would cause them to stumble. Give them the grace to lay these things at the altar and find Your perfect will, that they may be sincere without offense until the day of Messiah (Philippians 1:10).

DAY 28

I will tell of the decree: The LORD said to me, "You are my Son; today I have begotten you. Ask of me, and I will make the nations your heritage, and the ends of the earth your possession. You shall break them with a rod of iron and dash them in pieces like a potter's vessel."

Psalm 2:7–9

Remember that the shepherd boy, who stood with holy confidence before Goliath while King Saul and the army of Israel cowered in the background, is the author of this Psalm (see 1 Samuel 17). Refusing to wear the cumbersome armor of his day, David charged out to face Goliath. He didn't see *big* Goliath and *little* David as he ran toward the battle line. He didn't see a huge sword and a little slingshot. All he saw were the powers of darkness mocking and defying the living God. David's stone and sling were irrelevant. He had the name of the Lord of hosts and the unshakeable confidence that his God would prevail!

PRAYER STARTER

Father, give grace to believers in the land of Israel to be soldiers in Your great end-time army. O Lord, give them an unshakeable confidence in Your victory. Defeat the giants that try to intimidate them and try to cause them to forget Your awesome power and glory.

NIGHT 28

That you may be filled with the knowledge of His will in all wisdom and spiritual understanding; that you may have a walk worthy of the Lord, fully pleasing Him.
Colossians 1:9–10 (NKJV)

With hindsight, many people wonder why the church in Europe in the 1930s said very little in regard to the persecution of the Jews in their neighborhoods. How could they let their children's friends be taken away to unknown destinations? Why did they not do anything when the Jewish businesses were closed down or synagogues ransacked? Unless the Lord reveals the knowledge of His will and strengthens us, would we not do the same? Anti-Semitism is increasing in all parts of the world; there are even those who are openly calling for the removal of Israel from the face of the earth.

PRAYER STARTER

Father, we ask You to have mercy upon us, weak and fragile human beings. Have mercy on us when we act without regard to knowing Your will. Please show us, Father, how we should pray for the Jewish people, how we should speak up on their behalf when people speak against them. Give us wisdom when to speak and who to speak to in situations where the Jewish people are maligned. We long to have a walk worthy of You. We long to be pleasing to You at all times.

DAY 29

Now the eleven disciples went to Galilee, to the mountain to which Jesus had directed them. And when they saw him they worshiped him, but some doubted. And Jesus came and said to them, "All authority in heaven and on earth has been given to me. Go therefore and make disciples of all nations, baptizing them in the name of the Father and of the Son and of the Holy Spirit, teaching them to observe all that I have commanded you. And behold, I am with you always, to the end of the age."

Matthew 28:16–20

The Jewish disciples were instructed by their Jewish Messiah to preach, teach, baptize, and disciple the nations—to go, sent in His name. Consider how critical it is for the Jews to come to the brightness of His light (Isaiah 60:1–3), to be fully immersed in the understanding that Yeshua is Messiah and King over Israel, so that they will then understand their calling to be sent ones to the nations.

PRAYER STARTER

Abba Father, I pray in the name of Yeshua that all of Israel will turn to You and be saved. I see how important it is for the Jews to understand their hope and calling to be sent out as Your disciples to present the truth that will set all mankind free. For those who have already believed that Yeshua is Messiah, may they obey the call to share the Good News of Messiah to all the nations, in Jerusalem, Judea and Samaria—indeed, to the ends of the earth (Acts 1:8), so that all the world will see Yeshua high and lifted up.

NIGHT 29

In that day the remnant of Israel and the survivors of the house of Jacob will no more lean on him who struck them, but will lean on the LORD, the Holy One of Israel, in truth. A remnant will return, the remnant of Jacob, to the mighty God. For though your people Israel be as the sand of the sea, only a remnant of them will return.
Isaiah 10:20–22

The Lord has promised in His Word, more than once, that there will be a remnant of Jews who return to the Lord their God. These ones will know Yeshua as the Messiah and the Holy Son of God.

PRAYER STARTER
O Lord, save Your people, the remnant of Israel (Jeremiah 31:7).

DAY 30

You will seek me and find me, when you seek me with all your heart. I will be found by you, declares the LORD, and I will restore your fortunes and gather you from all the nations and all the places where I have driven you, declares the LORD, and I will bring you back to the place from which I sent you into exile.
Jeremiah 29:13–14

One reason God gave David only one-twelfth of the kingdom of Hebron was because He wanted David's core of fighting men, the future army of Israel, to become mature and seasoned. God wanted a core of submitted, committed leaders free of ambition. To their credit, these men became righteous warriors, using their strength for the greater glory of God and Israel instead of doing their own thing. They found the secret that working together produces far greater results than going it alone.

PRAYER STARTER

God of heaven's army, raise up righteous warriors like David's mighty men among the believers in Israel. Give them the grace to dwell together in unity. I ask for unity among believers, a unity that commands a blessing (Psalm 133).

NIGHT 30

For this reason I bow my knees before the Father, from whom every family in heaven and on earth is named, that according to the riches of his glory he may grant you to be strengthened with power through his Spirit in your inner being, so that Christ may dwell in your hearts through faith—that you, being rooted and grounded in love, may have strength to comprehend with all the saints what is the breadth and length and height and depth, and to know the love of Christ that surpasses knowledge, that you may be filled with all the fullness of God.
Ephesians 3:14–19

Being rooted and grounded in the strong, secure love of God will motivate believers to greater faithfulness, spiritual passion, and maturity. They will long for a fuller, more intimate knowledge of God and for heart-to-heart fellowship with Him. As they pursue intimacy with Yeshua, it will become apparent that they are God's children. They will manifest their family's likeness by conforming to Messiah. They will seek to further their family's welfare by loving their brethren. They will maintain their family's honor by avoiding what their Father hates, pursuing what He loves, and seeking His glory.

PRAYER STARTER

Father, root and ground believers in the land of Israel and throughout the Diaspora in Your everlasting love. Let them manifest Your likeness and live in purity and holiness as they show Your love to others.

DAY 31

For we will surely die and become like water spilled on the ground, which cannot be gathered up again. Yet God does not take away a life; but He devises means, so that His banished ones are not expelled from Him.
2 Samuel 14:14 (NKJV)

But if some of the branches were broken off, and you, although a wild olive shoot, were grafted in among the others and now share in the nourishing root of the olive tree, do not be arrogant toward the branches. If you are, remember it is not you who support the root, but the root that supports you.
Romans 11:17–18

Through Romans 11, we see that natural (Jewish) branches were broken off so that Gentile believers would be grafted into the living tree. Yet Paul tells us this is not a permanent condition. We know the God of covenant keeps His covenant to a thousand generations and that the root (Israel) supports the branches (Gentile believers). Israel will be grafted back in.

PRAYER STARTER

Father, we ask for You to graft back in many natural branches. Reveal Your Son, the Way, the Truth, and the Life, to the Jewish people. We long for the natural fruit from the natural branches.

NIGHT 31

Out of the depths I cry to you, O LORD! If you, O LORD, should mark iniquities, O Lord, who could stand? But with you there is forgiveness, that you may be feared. O Israel, hope in the LORD! For with the LORD there is steadfast love, and with him is plentiful redemption. And he will redeem Israel from all his iniquities.
Psalm 130:1, 3–4, 7–8

There is a deep cry that comes from within us when we realize that apart from God's mercy and forgiveness, all humanity is hopeless and destined for destruction. God is longing for His beloved Israel to put their hope in Him, that they would be forgiven and redeemed.

PRAYER STARTER
God, I ask that You would allow unbelieving Jewish people to feel the separation between Your holy nature and their sinful hearts. Enlighten their eyes to see Yeshua as the only solution and give them a cry within for mercy today.

DAY 32

Therefore do not fear, O My servant Jacob, says the LORD, nor be dismayed, O Israel; for behold, I will save you from afar, and your seed from the land of their captivity. Jacob shall return, have rest and be quiet, and no one shall make him afraid.

Jeremiah 30:10 (NKJV)

Fear is the enemy's primary way of working against humanity. In light of all they have suffered throughout history, the Jewish people of all people have every reason to be afraid. However, all of God's promises are "Yes and Amen" (2 Corinthians 1:20) and He promises to take fear from them.

PRAYER STARTER

We prophesy over Israel: "God did not give you a Spirit of fear, but of power, love, and sound mind" (2 Timothy 1:7). Father, I ask You to pour out Your Spirit on Israel and remove fear from her.

NIGHT 32

The LORD is my light and my salvation; whom shall I fear? The LORD is the stronghold of my life; of whom shall I be afraid? When evildoers assail me to eat up my flesh, my adversaries and foes, it is they who stumble and fall. Though an army encamp against me, my heart shall not fear; though war arise against me, yet I will be confident.
Psalm 27:1–3

The nation of Israel exists with armies encamped around her and the possibility of war breaking out each day. Yet, these are the kinsmen of David about whom he testified that he would continue to trust. David built a history of faith with God. Each time he stepped out of fear and into the strength and boldness of God, a new page was added to his personal book of faith. When the dark night comes and believers face great trouble, they can draw on their private history with God. The hearts of believers need not faint for fear like unbelievers. Rather, they can overcome fear through a personal history of His faithfulness.

PRAYER STARTER

Father, give believers in the land of Israel a personal history of faith. Let them look back upon their lives and see Your miraculous intervention and blessing. Let them agree with David's testimony and say, "I will not be afraid, because I remember that God has continually been my salvation and my deliverer."

DAY 33

And of Zion it shall be said, "This one and that one were born in her"; for the Most High himself will establish her. The LORD records as he registers the peoples, "This one was born there." . . . Singers and dancers alike say, "All my springs are in you."

Psalm 87:5–7

Oh, that salvation for Israel would come out of Zion!

Psalm 53:6

A *sabra* is a Jewish person who is born in Israel. Messianic *sabras* are to be salt and light (Matthew 5:13–16) for their Jewish brothers and sisters who have yet to believe in Yeshua.

PRAYER STARTER

We proclaim regarding the *sabras* and other Messianic believers in the land, "On that Day, when He comes to be glorified by His holy people and admired by all who have trusted, you will be among them. With this in view, we always pray for you that our God may make you worthy of His calling and may fulfill by His power every good purpose of yours and every action stemming from your trust. In this way, the name of our Lord Yeshua will be glorified in you, and you in Him, in accordance with the grace of our God and the Lord Yeshua the Messiah" (2 Thessalonians 1:10–12).

NIGHT 33

The Levites stood with the instruments of David, and the priests with the trumpets. Then Hezekiah commanded that the burnt offering be offered on the altar. And when the burnt offering began, the song to the LORD began also, and the trumpets, accompanied by the instruments of David king of Israel.
2 Chronicles 29:26–27

God has been releasing His songs throughout the centuries. The Scriptures exhort God's people to sing new songs unto the Lord. The Holy Sprit stands ready to anoint and inspire many prophetic musicians and singers who will discern the fresh music from heaven and release it to the body of believers for their enjoyment, refreshment, instruction, and admonition.

PRAYER STARTER

Holy Spirit, release the new songs in Your modern-day Levites who minister before You in prayer rooms and congregations throughout Israel. Let hearts burst forth with the fresh music of heaven. Raise up a symphony of prophetic musicians and singers to spread the songs of heaven in Israel.

DAY 34

Brothers, my heart's desire and prayer to God for them is that they may be saved.
Romans 10:1

The heart and emotions of many Holocaust survivors may best be described by the following quote from *At the Mind's Limits: Contemplations by a Survivor on Auschwitz and its Realities* by Jean Amery: "Being a Jew means feeling the tragedy of yesterday as an inner oppression. Without trust in the world I face my surroundings as a Jew who is alien and alone and all I can manage is to get along with this foreignness."

PRAYER STARTER

Abba, I ask You to pour out Your Spirit on those who have lived through the horrific conditions of the Holocaust. Give countless Holocaust survivors and their families dreams and visions of Your Son Yeshua, their Messiah. Give them eyes to see You, ears to hear You, and a heart to receive You. Abba, speak words of tender affection over their tired and weary hearts. Acquaint them with Yeshua, their Savior who bore their grief; their deliverer who carried their sorrows; the slain Lamb who takes away their transgressions. Abba, save Holocaust survivors today.

NIGHT 34

For it is impossible for the blood of bulls and goats to take away sins. Consequently, when Christ came into the world, he said, "Sacrifices and offerings you have not desired, but a body have you prepared for me; in burnt offerings and sin offerings you have taken no pleasure. Then I said, 'Behold, I have come to do your will, O God, as it is written of me in the scroll of the book.'"

Hebrews 10:4–7

Yeshua came to bear the wrath of God for our sins. When He completed His obedience unto death, God raised Him to life and seated Him on His throne. The sacrifices were a shadow of Yeshua's coming as the Lamb of God: "For it is impossible that the blood of bulls and goats should take away sins."

PRAYER STARTER

Holy God, I ask that You would overcome the ways in which the enemy and even the Church have distorted the message of the cross. Give Your Jewish people revelation of the cross: the agony of Yeshua's body, soul and spirit; the agony of the Father's heart as He gave His only Son; the working of the Holy Spirit to help Yeshua endure to the end. Show them there is no replacement for His blood! Let Your people know that the blood of Yeshua is the fulfillment of the old covenant promises. Make known Yeshua the Messiah and Him crucified. God, have mercy on us all for minimizing the shed blood of Your only Son.

DAY 35

Get you up to a high mountain, O Zion, herald of good news; lift up your voice with strength, O Jerusalem, herald of good news; lift it up, fear not; say to the cities of Judah, "Behold your God!" Behold, the Lord GOD comes with might, and his arm rules for him; behold, his reward is with him, and his recompense before him.
Isaiah 40:9–10

That you were enriched in everything by Him in all utterance and all knowledge, even as the testimony of Christ was confirmed in you.
1 Corinthians 1:5–6 (NKJV)

Two thousand years ago a small band of anointed believers turned history around in the nation of Israel. For the first time since the days of the early church, there are now 10,000 believing descendants of Abraham, Isaac, and Jacob in Israel. Let us pray that the Lord will anoint these believers, as He did when He poured out His Spirit on the day of Pentecost in Jerusalem, and that once again there will be a people who will change history with anointed preaching and teaching.

PRAYER STARTER

Father, I ask You to anoint every word that proceeds from the mouth of each believer in Israel through the preaching of the Word and the speaking of prophetic revelation to unbelievers. I pray that whenever they open their mouths, the words will be given to them to be bold in making known the mystery of the gospel (Ephesians 6:19). I pray that the Word of the Lord would not return void, but would change hearts when it is uttered.

NIGHT 35

Then he said to them, "These are my words that I spoke to you while I was still with you, that everything written about me in the Law of Moses and the Prophets and the Psalms must be fulfilled." Then he opened their minds to understand the Scriptures, and said to them, "Thus it is written, that the Christ should suffer and on the third day rise from the dead, and that repentance and forgiveness of sins should be proclaimed in his name to all nations, beginning from Jerusalem."

Luke 24:44–47

The message of Yeshua can be clearly found in the *Torah*, Prophets, and Psalms. As the Jewish people read their Hebrew scriptures, let us pray that they gain understanding to see their Messiah.

PRAYER STARTER

Father, let the Word that has come from Your mouth not return unfulfilled. As Your people read the *Torah*, Prophets, and Psalms, let Your Word accomplish what You intend and cause to succeed what You sent it to do (Isaiah 55:11). I ask God, that Your Jewish people may have all the riches that come from understanding and fully knowing Your secret truth, which is the Messiah (Colossians 2:2).

DAY 36

Who is on the LORD's side? Come to me.
Exodus 32:26

But the Levitical priests, the sons of Zadok, who kept the charge of my sanctuary when the people of Israel went astray from me, shall come near to me to minister to me . . . They shall enter my sanctuary, and they shall approach my table, to minister to me, and they shall keep my charge.
Ezekiel 44:15–16

Israel is in desperate need of a priesthood of believers like the sons of Zadok: men and women who will see the unrighteous acts of their nation Israel, separate themselves, and draw near to the Lord and His righteousness. These are the ones who will minister to God's heart on behalf of the people.

PRAYER STARTER

God, give Your priests grace to stir up Your jealousy for Your land and Your mercy for Your people. Let the priests, the ministers of the LORD, weep and say, "Spare Your people, O LORD, and make not Your heritage a reproach, a byword among the nations. Why should they say among the peoples, 'Where is their God?'" (Joel 2:17–18).

NIGHT 36

And the LORD said to him, "Pass through the city, through Jerusalem, and put a mark on the foreheads of the men who sigh and groan over all the abominations that are committed in it."

Ezekiel 9:4

No city is or ever has been perfectly righteous. Even so, God has chosen a city for His Son to return to and to reign; that city is Jerusalem. In preparation for His return, there will be a great separation of the wheat and the tares: those who love truth and righteousness, and those who love deception and wickedness. God knows those who belong to Him and He will make a distinction between His sheep—those who cry out over sin and unrighteousness—and the goats of the world.

PRAYER STARTER

Lord God, tenderize people's hearts even now in the city of Jerusalem. Let the light of the witness of Yeshua, the Messiah, shine in the hearts of those dwelling there. God, we ask that You would have mercy on Jerusalem; find and capture every heart that groans over the wickedness done in that city. Mark them now. Place Your seal upon them. Cleanse and purge Your city of unrighteousness and make a way for Your Son to enter into those gates once more with shouts of "Blessed is He who comes in the name of the LORD!" (Psalm 118:26).

DAY 37

I call heaven and earth to witness against you today, that I have set before you life and death, blessing and curse. Therefore choose life, that you and your offspring may live, loving the LORD your God, obeying his voice and holding fast to him, for he is your life and length of days, that you may dwell in the land that the LORD swore to your fathers, to Abraham, to Isaac, and to Jacob, to give them.
Deuteronomy 30:19–20

Two million babies were aborted in the first sixty years of modern-day Israel's existence. This is a significant number when compared to the national population of seven million people. Israel permits legal abortion up until the ninth month of pregnancy, and female soldiers in the Israeli Defense Force are given two free abortions during their two years of mandatory service. Fewer Jewish children died in the Holocaust (1.5 million children) than at the hands of abortion doctors within the land of Israel.

PRAYER STARTER

God, You are a Father and You call Your people children. Open up the eyes of Jewish men and women. Show them that the child in the womb is precious in Your sight, and that You have a wonderful calling for each one. Let them choose life so that they will live!

NIGHT 37

For the mystery of lawlessness is already at work. Only he who now restrains it will do so until he is out of the way. And then the lawless one will be revealed, whom the Lord Jesus will kill with the breath of his mouth and bring to nothing by the appearance of his coming.
2 Thessalonians 2:7–8

In reading these verses we understand the forewarning that a season of lawlessness will come, and, even now, is upon the earth; this includes hatred of the Jewish people and those who support the hope of their calling. We must pray fervently that the Holy Spirit, God's heavenly restrainer, will suppress and foil this explosion of anti-Semitism in our day.

PRAYER STARTER

Dear Captain of the Lord of Hosts, I see and know that the enemy is raging and manifesting through a spirit of lawlessness and a hatred of the Jews. Even though You have forewarned us about this season, in the name of Your Holy Son Yeshua, I ask for You to shed light in the darkness. May the revelation of the love of our Jewish Messiah shatter the lies and expose the truth. Sustain the Jewish people and let them also see Your light.

DAY 38

Alas! That day is so great there is none like it; it is a time of distress for Jacob; yet he shall be saved out of it.
Jeremiah 30:7

At first glance Jeremiah Chapter 30 seems like very bad news for the Jewish people. Yet in this chapter alone, there are seventeen "I will" promises from God! He promises to save Jacob and give him rest from all his troubles. And what He says, He will do.

PRAYER STARTER

Abba, no matter how difficult it gets for the Jewish people, let this be their confession: "But in my mind I keep returning to something, something that gives me hope—that the grace of the Lord is not exhausted, that His compassion has not ended. His mercies are new every morning! How great is His faithfulness!" (Lamentations 3:21–23).

NIGHT 38

One thing have I asked of the LORD, that will I seek after: that I may dwell in the house of the LORD all the days of my life, to gaze upon the beauty of the LORD and to inquire in his temple. For he will hide me in his shelter in the day of trouble; he will conceal me under the cover of his tent; he will lift me high upon a rock. And now my head shall be lifted up above my enemies all around me, and I will offer in his tent sacrifices with shouts of joy; I will sing and make melody to the LORD. Hear, O LORD, when I cry aloud; be gracious to me and answer me! You have said, "Seek my face." My heart says to you, "Your face, LORD, do I seek."
Psalms 27:4–8

What is the path to overcoming great fear in the midst of great trouble? David's example makes it clear: he overcame fear by seeking God's face in intimacy; he gazed upon the heart of God, encountering His beauty. Throughout his life, David was pursued by those determined to destroy him. Yet in response to these trials, David proclaimed that God would hide him in His shelter. His example of trust in God illuminates the way Jewish believers are to posture their hearts in the midst of persecution and trouble.

PRAYER STARTER

Father, keep Jewish believers in the land from fear of what others might say or do to them. Keep them from feeling the sting of rejection and hatred from others. When evildoers threaten to destroy them, let them overcome evil by living in the security of Your love. Give Jewish believers grace to gaze on Your beauty and dwell in Your house.

DAY 39

This is what the Lord GOD showed me: behold, the Lord GOD was calling for a judgment by fire, and it devoured the great deep and was eating up the land. Then I said, "O Lord GOD, please cease! How can Jacob stand? He is so small!" The LORD relented concerning this: "This also shall not be," said the Lord GOD.

Amos 7:4–6

God revealed to Amos that He was preparing to release impending judgment against Israel. Amos cried "No!" He appealed to God to consider the smallness and fragility of His very own people, and God relented. Today, let consider the smallness and fragility of the nation of Israel (the size of New Jersey, with a population of only 5.5 million Jewish people) positioned amidst nations calling for her destruction. Again, let us cry to God: "Look how small she is—spare her!"

PRAYER STARTER

Father, we ask You to look upon Your people again and consider the schemes of those who would bring her down. God, we ask You to frustrate the schemes of evil men bent upon her destruction. Intervene again on behalf of Israel and let her recognize You as her Deliverer.

NIGHT 38

One thing have I asked of the LORD, that will I seek after: that I may dwell in the house of the LORD all the days of my life, to gaze upon the beauty of the LORD and to inquire in his temple. For he will hide me in his shelter in the day of trouble; he will conceal me under the cover of his tent; he will lift me high upon a rock. And now my head shall be lifted up above my enemies all around me, and I will offer in his tent sacrifices with shouts of joy; I will sing and make melody to the LORD. Hear, O LORD, when I cry aloud; be gracious to me and answer me! You have said, "Seek my face." My heart says to you, "Your face, LORD, do I seek."
Psalms 27:4–8

What is the path to overcoming great fear in the midst of great trouble? David's example makes it clear: he overcame fear by seeking God's face in intimacy; he gazed upon the heart of God, encountering His beauty. Throughout his life, David was pursued by those determined to destroy him. Yet in response to these trials, David proclaimed that God would hide him in His shelter. His example of trust in God illuminates the way Jewish believers are to posture their hearts in the midst of persecution and trouble.

PRAYER STARTER

Father, keep Jewish believers in the land from fear of what others might say or do to them. Keep them from feeling the sting of rejection and hatred from others. When evildoers threaten to destroy them, let them overcome evil by living in the security of Your love. Give Jewish believers grace to gaze on Your beauty and dwell in Your house.

DAY 39

This is what the Lord GOD showed me: behold, the Lord GOD was calling for a judgment by fire, and it devoured the great deep and was eating up the land. Then I said, "O Lord GOD, please cease! How can Jacob stand? He is so small!" The LORD relented concerning this: "This also shall not be," said the Lord GOD.

Amos 7:4–6

God revealed to Amos that He was preparing to release impending judgment against Israel. Amos cried "No!" He appealed to God to consider the smallness and fragility of His very own people, and God relented. Today, let consider the smallness and fragility of the nation of Israel (the size of New Jersey, with a population of only 5.5 million Jewish people) positioned amidst nations calling for her destruction. Again, let us cry to God: "Look how small she is—spare her!"

PRAYER STARTER

Father, we ask You to look upon Your people again and consider the schemes of those who would bring her down. God, we ask You to frustrate the schemes of evil men bent upon her destruction. Intervene again on behalf of Israel and let her recognize You as her Deliverer.

NIGHT 39

Behold, my servant shall act wisely; he shall be high and lifted up, and shall be exalted. As many were astonished at you—his appearance was so marred, beyond human semblance, and his form beyond that of the children of mankind—so shall he sprinkle many nations; kings shall shut their mouths because of him; for that which has not been told them they see, and that which they have not heard they understand.
Isaiah 52:13–15

As for me, I have set my King on Zion, my holy hill.
Psalm 2:6

Yeshua sits on the throne in heaven, and it is God's will that He should one day sit on a throne here on earth. That throne will be on the Temple Mount on Mount Zion in Jerusalem. God Himself will see to it that His Son sits on that throne.

PRAYER STARTER

Our Father in heaven, may Your Name be kept holy. May Your Kingdom come, Your will be done on earth as in heaven (Matthew 6:10). Enthrone Your Son in Jerusalem. The Spirit and the Bride say, "Come!" Even so, come, Lord Yeshua!

DAY 40

So Joseph said to his brothers, "Come near to me, please."
                                            Genesis 45:4

And I will pour out on the house of David and the inhabitants of Jerusalem a spirit of grace and pleas for mercy, so that, when they look on me, on him whom they have pierced, they shall mourn for him, as one mourns for an only child, and weep bitterly over him, as one weeps over a firstborn.
                                            Zechariah 12:10

As with Joseph, there will be a time when the identity of Yeshua is revealed to His brothers. On that day, all the inhabitants of Jerusalem will mourn in repentance as they see Yeshua face to face. By the power of the Holy Spirit touching their hearts, all Israel will look at Him and recognize Him as their Savior and Messiah.

PRAYER STARTER

God of Israel, pour out Your grace over the city of Jerusalem today, and awaken a cry in the hearts of the Jewish people as You reveal Your Son Yeshua to them as their Savior and Messiah. Yeshua, call Your people to come closer, that they may recognize You as their brother and Messiah. Make Your face shine and they will be saved (Psalm 80:3, 7, 19).

NIGHT 40

These I will bring to my holy mountain, and make them joyful in my house of prayer; their burnt offerings and their sacrifices will be accepted on my altar; for my house shall be called a house of prayer for all peoples.
Isaiah 56:7

David was consumed with zeal for the house of God. This vision so consumed him that he established a night-and-day prophetic worship ministry to the Lord with four thousand musicians and two hundred eighty-eight singers (1 Chronicles 23–25). Throughout the generations, there has been an expression of night-and-day prayer in the nations of the earth, for God has said, "My house will be called a house of prayer for all nations."

PRAYER STARTER

Father, strengthen the houses of prayer and prayer rooms in Israel. Raise up Israeli singers, musicians, and intercessors who will minister before You day and night.